HIGH SCHOOL ISN'T PRETTY

HIGH SCHOOL ISN'T PRETTY

JOHN McPHERSON

Andrews and McMeel
A Universal Press Syndicate Company
Kansas City

Library of Congress Catalog Card Number: 93-71861

ISBN: 0-8362-1728-4

00 01 QUK 10 9 8

———————————— ATTENTION: SCHOOLS AND BUSINESSES ————————————

Andrews and McMeel books are available at quantity discounts with bulk purchase for educational, business, or sales promotional use. For information, write to: Special Sales Department, Andrews and McMeel, 4520 Main Street, Kansas City, Missouri 64111.

To Beth

HITTING THE BOOKS

"Good morning, and welcome to introduction to chemistry."

"Cosgrove! Get back here!"

"Bummer of a locker assignment, Walt."

Basically, Bob didn't have a clue what courses he was taking or where he was supposed to be.

Needless to say, people were extremely psyched about the school's new vending machine.

"Sorry. I had this overwhelming urge to put it in reverse while we were going 55."

"Did you just say 'Ribbit'?!"

"Man, did you scare me! For a second there I thought you were my math teacher!"

Set design wasn't exactly a priority with the Binkler High Drama Club.

Veteran bus driver Norm Putzer didn't have too much sympathy for anyone who was late for the bus.

Tina Rumford discovered that gravy from the school's cafeteria makes great tanning lotion.

Mike hoped that Mr. Wester would take into account the realism of his volcano project as he graded it.

16

Brenda Lasman lucks into getting the one and only locker number 582.

"He's been getting on my nerves ever since he took that speed reading course."

"You forgot your locker combination again, didn't you?"

"Ron, I'm your lab partner. Trust me."

"Personally, I think this new attendance system stinks."

Wes Lunker uses a visual aid to enhance his report on the planets.

"I hope this won't affect my grade."

High School goes high-tech with the onset of the remote control locker opener.

"Well, at last we have a volunteer to do the oral report on osmosis."

25

"Sorry, we're out of plates."

"Would you watch where you're going?!
You're standing on my earring!"

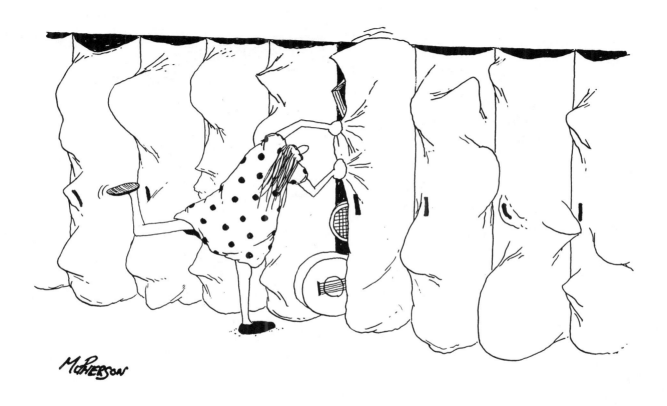

The latest breakthrough in locker technology: elastic doors.

"Man, you shouldn't have drank that stuff. Now Coach probably won't let you start in the game Friday night."

28

Somehow, the Fegley High Drama Club's presentation of *Jaws* didn't quite measure up to the movie version.

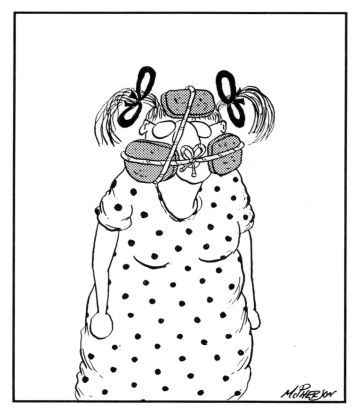

Louise Magnarski tests her theory that cafeteria meat-loaf can cure acne.

"I've got a feeling this isn't going to do wonders for our lab grades."

"Personally, I liked the old school bus better."

"I think I'll be brown-bagging it from now on!"

Warren Pelnard demonstrates his combination napkin holder and bird feeder.

33

Two upperclassmen attempt to break a school record by stuffing thirteen freshmen into a locker.

"Sorry, sir. I saw one of those woolly caterpillars in the road back there and I didn't want to hit it."

The year the S.A.T. creators decided to mess with students' minds.

After 17 years as a home ec. teacher, Edwina Kratz
was having a tough time settling in as a chemistry teacher.

**The third period chem. class discovered that the rubber tubing
used in the lab is great for bungee jumping.**

Wes Fumple had gotten downright lazy when it came to taking notes.

Linda Batsky had watched too much "Wheel of Fortune."

School librarian Nelda Limpkin was pretty pleased with her new book classifying system.

The hazards of wearing too much make-up.

"A food fight? Not that I know of, sir. Oh, wait. Dale Musner did spill a carton of milk. Is that what you're thinking of?"

Unable to find guys who could dance in the school musical, choreographer Nelda Crantz develops and tests her automatic dancing machine.

**Apparently Louise Bamford had never heard the age-old test advice:
Stick with your first answer.**

"Sorry, sir. I didn't see that cattle crossing sign until it was too late."

"Mike made these for me in metal shop."

For the sake of convenience, the school nurse's office was relocated
next to home economics.

Students at Milfoil High weren't too fond of the new hall passes.

For a great practical joke, substitute some Kool-Aid for your chemistry experiment, then drink it.

"All you had to do was follow the float with the pink cows! Was that so hard?!"

"You gotta admit, it's pretty refreshing compared to the graffiti
we've had around here in the past."

Terrifying freshmen on the first day of school is a favorite pastime of many seniors.

Biology students study samples taken from a
school drinking fountain.

As head of the school safety committee
Mrs. Snedman did her best to discourage students
from running in the halls.

"I'm tellin' ya, there's something weird about that new guy."

Talking report cards: proof that technology is not always good.

This particular incident, involving the fifth period wood shop class, had a lot to do with Mrs. Lunk's sudden retirement.

Years of people sticking their gum under desks were starting to take their toll.

Students at Lifner High were let down when they found out that their foreign exchange student was from Ohio.

It was an ironic ending to Mr. Slasky's slide presentation on safety.

"I think it's time I had a little talk
with my locker mate."

Although the new graduation process at
Burnsville High was faster, it didn't quite have the
glamour of the traditional graduation ceremony.

Timing is an essential part of being a yearbook photographer.

Wayne was deeply touched by the personal inscriptions in his yearbook.

SPORTS

"All right. That's enough stretching out. Let's play some ball!"

In an effort to reduce injuries, the Clodpell Valley Football Conference
devised the two-hand tickle tackling rule.

63

The spirit of Christmas caused a rare display of generosity by gym teacher Art Mankowski.

Thurston High couldn't afford a trampoline.

Marty and Bill were sick and tired of getting picked last in gym class.

Sliding was not Gordon's strong point.

Tired of the embarrassment of dropping batons during a routine, the Nelbert High Majorettes turned to the new gas-powered batons.

Told that he was too short to play basketball, Warren soon began proving his critics wrong.

Although intended to boost the team's morale, coach Finkley's reward system for making a basket actually had the reverse effect.

Although the glove was tough to maneuver, Mark hadn't missed a fly ball since his sophomore year.

Apparently there was some confusion as to exactly when during the game the Fegley High Marching Band was supposed to perform.

Slagmont High's mobile cheering section had a tremendous impact on their runners' morale.

In an attempt to combine sports and academics, officials at Culver High devised aerobic algebra.

The Binkler High hockey team's enthusiasm died down pretty quickly once they found out that the puck they just scored with was actually Wade Clingburn's retainer.

The new five-point shot created by the Wulby County Division Three Basketball Conference added a lot of excitement, despite the fact that no one had ever made one.

Having run out of stockings to decorate all of the lockers at Gupner High, the Christmas decorating committee was forced to finish the job using gym socks.

Majorettes make lousy relay racers.

For safety reasons, the **Watney High** athletic department
had air bags installed in the team's uniforms.

People were starting to think that home economics teacher Selma Lavitz wasn't the best choice to fill the assistant coaching position.

Wendy Skylar knew how to intimidate her opponents in the 100-meter butterfly.

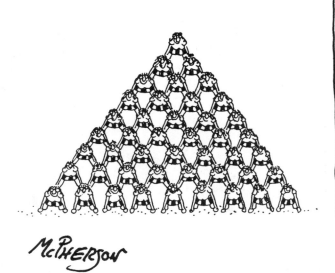

"Sorry, I had an itch."

"When you said your wheels were parked outside
I sort of thought you meant a car."

79

Always a practical joker, the rubber leg that Diane kept in her purse livened up many a first date.

On their first date, Bud takes Linda on a rousing tour
of the National Comb Museum.

"Why must you torture blind dates like this?!"

"Sorry about this, Diane. I could've sworn that door at the back of the theater was an exit."

83

Carl prided himself in keeping dating costs to a minimum.

Eliminate the hassle of deciding what to do on your next big date with the Date-O-Matic.

Obviously there was some misunderstanding about where Ray and Wanda were going on their date.

The girls at Mutler High were getting desperate.

"All I did was loan you a pencil in math class!
That doesn't mean we're going steady!"

Bob carries chivalry too far.

Wade didn't let the fact that the drive-in was closed keep him and Janet from having that unique drive-in experience.

**When he realized he'd forgotten a corsage for his prom date,
Norm quickly grabbed one of his mom's rosebushes.**

It took a lot of self-resistance for Luann to keep from picking up the phone, but she knew it was for the best.

Andy tried to subtly let Glenda know that she wore enough perfume to choke a rhino.

In their never-ending search for creative social events, the prom committee at Muldoon High devised the come-as-your-favorite major appliance dinner and dance.

WE NEED TO KNOW YOUR PARENTS' INCOME, YOUR EXPECTED SUMMER EARNINGS, YOUR TOTAL EARNINGS SINCE THE AGE OF TWO, THE AVERAGE INCOME OF ALL YOUR FIRST COUSINS, YOUR FATHER'S BARBER'S TOTAL ASSETS, 17 FORMS OF I.D., 131 PERSONAL REFERENCES,...
ETHEL LUNKLER
FINANCIAL AID ADVISOR
McPherson

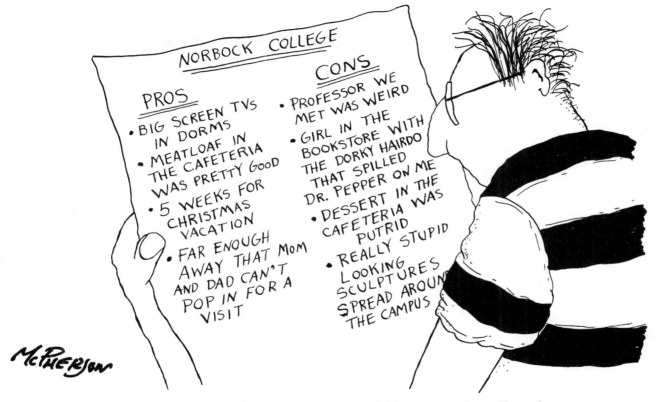

After visiting a college, it's a good idea to make a list of its positive and negative points.

"And here's our freshmen dorm! I'd take you through it but they're ... uh ... refinishing the solid oak floors."

Muckner College was known for its tough entrance interviews.

PAGE 137

APPLICATION FOR ENROLLMENT IN SPUDZBO COLLEGE.

456. IN 40,000 TO 60,000 WORDS, PLEASE TELL US WHY YOU WISH TO ATTEND SPUDZBO COLLEGE, WHAT PERSON IN HISTORY YOU ADMIRE MOST, WHAT YOU HOPE TO BE DOING IN 10 YEARS, AND HOW YOU WOULD SOLVE THE WORLD'S POPULATION CRISIS. (USE ADDITIONAL PAPER IF NECESSARY.)

457. PLEASE LIST 200 REFERENC WHO CAN VERIFY THAT YOU ARE NOT WEIRD.

Walt was starting to think he should have chosen a smaller college.

Learning to do your own laundry is a fundamental part of life as a college freshman.

A good college course will push students to their intellectual limits.

Freshman Lisa Dubner hadn't caught on to the fact that most college classes are held every other day.

Larry should have known better than to have signed up for an economy dorm room.

Stella's roommate had a tendency to be a bit territorial.

The size of some university libraries can be pretty
intimidating to first-year students.